Dynamite on a China Plate

Dynamite on a China Plate

P · O · E · M · S

BY JAY LEEMING

THE BACKWATERS PRESS

OMAHA, NEBRASKA

First printing, 2006

Designed by Richard E. Rosenbaum
Cover design by Bristol Creative
Cover art is a detail from *Abstract in Red: Consider the Leaf* by Ethel Vrana
Author photo copyright © 2005, Chris Leeming

Published by the Backwaters Press
3502 North 52nd Street
Omaha, NE 68104–3506

www. thebackwaterspress.homestead.com
gkosm62735@aol.com
(402) 451–4052

ISBN: 0–9765231–3–2

Printed and bound in the United States of America

Contents

PART ONE

THE BARBER

The barber is someone who creates
by taking away, like a writer
who owns only an eraser.
He is like a construction company

that begins with a large office building
and ends up with a small wooden house.
On the wall is his license,
showing that he's been to school

and learned of all the varieties
of loss. For this reason
a haircut can make me nervous;
sometimes I close my eyes

and hear only the snip
of the scissors, their two gleaming halves
talking of the balance that is here, the partnership
between this man in a blue smock

and the hairs faithful as rain,
that even before birth and after death
flow tirelessly out of the head
towards the comb and the blade.

APPLE

Sometimes when eating an apple
I bite too far
and open the little room
the lovers have prepared,
and the seeds fall
onto the kitchen floor
and I see
that they are tear-shaped.

RED AUTUMN BELLS

While holding her in my arms I start to think forward
and back, to number each chocolate, to throw rope
around laughter and her eyes.
But wondering how long it will last
is the best way to lose something
that's all yours. So I clamber back up
into the kiss, into this blue room
where we murmur together,
the two of us
becoming one river. Ankles, elbows,
eyes and thighs: we make one river.

I Want to Go Back

I want to go back beyond the chicken bones
and the piled garbage bags of Brooklyn in August,
back beyond the ring on her finger
and the party years ago
where I met her fierce, unpleasant husband
for the first time;
back beyond even the warm confusion
of her long body and blonde hair
on the bare mattress of a Saturday;
back to the moment when we lay down sweating
in the cricket-heavy darkness
with our heads together
and the music of the dance we'd left
burning just out of reach behind the trees,
to when we did nothing but breathe
as the northern lights
loosened their vapors across the stars.

Taking a Bath

Wonderful that world
when your ears go under,
when all you feel
is the ringing in the shell,
the bones' chorus,
and the melody
of birth.

MIDDLE OF THE NIGHT

The whistle of my parents' breath
as I stood in my pajamas
on the hairy carpet:
it reminded me of a moon-colored wheel
turning, something like the smooth disc
of the hand-drill in my father's workshop,
how it whirred and whispered. At six years old
getting up to go to the bathroom
meant this walk through the dark house
and across the windy square of their sleep, amazed
that I could listen to breath arriving
and arriving in the bodies out of which
I was born.

THE BEAMS OF MY PARENTS' HOUSE

The beams of this house were cut
with a two-handled saw: a slippery, scribbled
whing of a blade
that must be rhythmed into straightness
by two men working back and forth,
sweating, each listening with his arms
for the pause at the end
of the other's pull, the sleep
out of which he can drag the teeth
again through the tree, shedding its winters
into the grass. I can feel with my hand
each parallel cut that saw made, in 1810,
as Jefferson looked out the windows
of the White House, as the ashes of Indian villages
cooled in the hills. These beams
carried my weight as I grew, carried my brother
as he walked in his sleep, my father as he smoked
in his yellow chair, my mother
as she folded our clothes. Thirty years old
and home for the weekend
I think of what has supported me,
I stand in the basement and look up
at these rough, coffee-colored beams.

Rowboat

An oar is a paddle with a home. This arrangement seems awkward at first, as if it were wrong; the wood knocks in the oarlock, and would much rather be a church steeple, or the propeller of an old airplane in France. Yet as it bites deep into the wave it settles down, deciding that the axe and the carpenter were right. And you, too, are supposed to be sitting this way, back turned to what you want, watching your history unravel across the waves as your legs brush against the gunnels. Your feet are restless, wanting to be more involved. But your back is what gets you there, closer to what finally surprises you from behind: waves lapping at the shore, the soft nuzzle of sand.

Typing Class

In typing class we learn what the letter "B" feels like, and how even emptiness must be written. Our teacher paces at the front of the room and cries out: "J-A-space, J-S-space, J-D-space." She is not singing, she is not calling us to prayer or giving a speech or reciting Shakespeare. This is typing class, where we learn skills we can get paid for, such as typing business letters. *Dear Sir or Madam. I am in typing class. The quick brown fox jumps over the lazy dog. Yours Sincerely.* At the beginning of the semester, our hesitant taps at the keys sound like the first drops of rain on a roof. But after a few weeks we have real thunder going, our fingers snapping out the alphabet, all of us together creating the sound of a busy newsroom. The letters right under your fingertips are animals who have wandered blindly into the cage; all you have to do is close the door. But others you have to reach for. A capital "P" requires both hands, it's like stretching to grasp the jar of molasses at the back of the kitchen shelf. A "Z" is even more difficult; it's a shelf higher, you need a chair. And the numbers at the top of the keyboard are in another room entirely, maybe even in a cardboard box out in the garage. "Don't look down," the teacher says, as though we were mountain climbers. But there's no danger of falling. A bell rings at the edge of the page and at the end of the class. We hand in our business letters, and our teacher looks at them and gives them back to us the next day, after writing a letter at the top of each one.

COPIER

It hums and blasts and waits. It is very quiet
for a machine that eats trees; but then
it doesn't really, only holding their thin slices close
long enough to tell them all our plans.
Its cover and glass plate
are really a mouth and an ear that whisper
when you close them. But tell it
everything, for its secret
is forgetfulness, and the darkness it needs
to make its brief, flat day.

FEEDBACK
for Pete Townshend

If you hold the guitar close
to the amplifier's shivering weight
its sound comes back, the lower pitches falling away
to leave the one
climbing angel, the shimmer of the note
in a high mirror.
In bars and basements I hunted
that animal, that electric, discarded star—
above the foundation-stones of the bass and drums
the chipped Stratocaster flickered and strained.
My chest shook. I held the note
until it sang again.

LAMENT OF THE RECORDING ENGINEER

All the music I make turns to stone.
It lasts but does not breathe.
I love and hate this dance
which makes an enemy of the dust,
and ties tears
onto wheels of brown tape.

Give me the dangerous violin, risking every note
like dynamite on a china plate;
give me the story that burns up as it finishes,
the melody leaping out
onto its wire.

The crowd gasps.

Now roses will pour out of words
or we will ruin everything.

Exit, with Moose

A moose walks into the living room, and stands among my family drinking cocktails. We put down our glasses. This is why the vines have been coming in the kitchen windows, why last week the bathroom ceiling fell in. Brother gets into the car, then mother, father; with only a suitcase full of ribbons I am ready to go. The moose can have the house now. My foot is on fire, and the moon is in the backyard singing. Get up from the poem. Get up before it's too late, walk with your lamp off through the fields of the first light, to where the birds sing in the dark, and the dew is on the grass.

PART TWO

At Golgotha

Slowly the crowd grew tired of their own jeers
and began to leave. I swallowed,
tasting vinegar again. The few that remained
prayed on the ground below me,
clenching and unclenching their hands.
I noticed the sky, like a large animal
that had suddenly moved closer.
Then the first breath came. I remembered
the wooden boat shaking over the rapids
of the river's mouth, bumping
at the sea's gate. I remembered
running my hands over a newly
sanded board. . . Then the second breath
and a singing as of wheels or leaves,
and I felt the clay pot
shatter, the great wings kick once
like a new heart. Then the third breath
gripped my body down through muscle
and bone to the small bell
of my birth, and I was gone.

HE BREATHES OUT SLOWLY

A woman's lips are like dynamite, they can blow
a house right off its foundations, remove
the car from the garage, money out of
pockets, his watch, keys, coins and cards
thrown onto a table near half-empty drinks,
damp napkins and cigarettes touched with lipstick
like a red glow at dawn, leaving his house
he goes out to meet her
by the morning glories, flowers opening
to fill his life with dresses, earrings,
painted toenails, green shoes and a skirt
tumbling like black water and mirrors, a skirt
that spends the night beside a chair, on the floor
like the feather of a bird dropped,
the sound of their voices laughing together
heard through a wall
by a man watching TV alone,
their breath at night rippling out
in stories told to friends,
the ice cream they eat
by the water, watching ships he tells
the door slammed, I meant to tell you
when it was all over, I meant to say
just how we met and what it came to,
what I did, a sock beneath
a bed, a voice inside a violin, hand
on her back, the waltz wrapped
in the hat he left behind a chair.

CROWS

The cry of the crow is a jack-knife opening,
a traffic light turning from green
to black. Crows remember the granite blocks
lifted by slaves, the soldier's teeth grinding
as his scalp is removed. They are older
than the pads between the bones of the spine, creaking
in their boats up in the treetops, cackling like first frost,
an abandoned barn, a tractor rusting
in tall grass. Crows remember the nails
in Jesus' hands, the name of every prisoner killed
in the Colosseum, the poisoned cup, books burning
on the steps of the cathedral. Their call
swallows the priest's footsteps
as he walks away, swallows
the roar of the elephant, swallows even the sunlight
in the cherry lollipop
a small girl licks. Their cries shrink the world down
into a flour-dust of stars inside a cow's eyeball
rolling on wooden floorboards.
The crow
takes the world in its beak
flies to the top of the tallest tree
and won't come down.

DREAM OF RUSSIA

Horowitz sits in his hotel room, looking out
at the river bordered in white stone buildings. Pages of music
rest in his suitcase, notes waiting like birds in trees
or faces in a theater. Then white lightning:

tonight he will play for the Premier, for generals
and rich men. When the river freezes
children come to skate on its glass. The war
lies bruised and asleep in its wire cage

but still the State jaws scientists
until raw. Our fathers wear fur hats
and tell stories of a war
with no easy end. Shouting in the streets

has brought bricks enough for everyone,
a fire named Stalin that burns the hayfield
down to its roots. A chicken factory
with no roads to reach it. Cabbage

and dead horses. In the cold a violin plays
like two ice cubes rubbing together. Two hundred years
without a phone. Trains run backwards
beneath hotel clocks, and families

trust no one. She bakes bread
in a cruel gymnasium; bullets for brothers
as if they were crows. Now
we must eat the black spoons.

What is the Door

What is the door ringed with fangs
that has an eye looking out of its keyhole?

It is a door that says "I've locked the rabbits
in a lead shoe. I've blown out the candle
in the flower. Talk to me."

And the window made of ribs, the window swallowing a clock
that tries to ring, but can't?

It is a bullet that shoots guns, it is a knife
that cuts knives. It is a hospital with no beds
and a small boy curled up on the floor.

What is the lighthouse that buzzes like a trapped fly,
with chains on its stairs
and a green flower glowing at its top?

It is a stomach grumbling about fathers.
It is a woman's hair when she is asleep.
It is a payphone ringing in the skull.
It is an empty school bus driving up the bones.
It is a red butterfly inside a suit of armor.
It is a camera that sees everything.
It is a map to a place we must go to
that does not exist.

Six Colors

Green for what you want; green for the ballroom
and the salt on the kitchen stairs. Green
for the jukebox, for onions and telephones
and the sand that fills up the shells.

Red for the dog's bark, for the roots
of rhubarb, for the angel that watches
over the bowling alley. Red for the general
and his rockets falling into the sea.

Blue for the hermit in his cave
with the moon in a bowl; blue
for the horse in a dream, for the gravestone
of ants, the photo of grandmother as a child.

Yellow for binoculars and shouting, yellow
for the opera that begins with a wine bottle
opened in an attic, yellow for lost money
and the ambassador thrown out a window.

White for papers sleeping in filing cabinets, and for tour buses
driven over hunting grounds; white for the faucet
that coughs blood, and the dice
that do not know victory or defeat.

Black for the inside of the box when
it is closed. Black for the parachute
that might open, for the ice on which
the day is built. Black for the shovels the elk hear

as they move deeper, like music, into the mountains.

Part Three

The Comedian's Ten Songs

1.

The race begins the cars slamming like tight knots
of white stars Jones in the lead Williams
close at the far turn a red blur pow
one million dollars gas smoke lightning

oh the quiet oak tree and the sleep of the dead.
How the torn papers rustle in the wind. United as one
the crowd looks from right to left give me
the car keys I'm going home to read books

2.

He spoke a foreign language, as he stood at the end
of the creaking dock with the sun shouting
music in the waves, with the seaweed mouthing
its dry chorus on the beach. Police broke down

the door of apartment 5B just to hear
the Clown's jokes. But he spoke a foreign language
standing at the end of the creaking dock
as the fish in their silence came nearer

3.

Here in The Building you can listen to the sound of money a sound
like a thousand stairs The Company wants very much
to know what America wants what women
ages eighteen to thirty-four are watching what

young single men are most likely to turn on
and rip to pieces with their bare hands
a bag of Doritos crinkles in Ohio's beer-soaked room
the Marketing Director's helicopter leaves the ground

4.

And the railroad, Your Majesty; and my vast
collection of iron nails, Mr. President.
Indeed my supper dish, Your Excellency; and most certainly
the sinkhole into which the crumbling stadium fell.

But the green candle, Mr. Secretary;
but the wet log, Madam Chairwoman. And might I add
the twisted hulk of a burned charcoal Volkswagen.
Yet the velvet telephone, Mr. Senator. . .

5.

When at last we reached the north pole its sound drowned
us in a black magnetic buzz, soaking
our boots and jackets in why-had-we-come.
A summer's day hunted us from inside even the smallest

piece of ice. Our sleds were loaded down with
the twelve tons of fear it takes to build
one cup of coffee. The world was searchlights and white statues,
money and dead bread. Our dogs slept.

6.

The Clown takes the soft hand of the Harp Player in his own
and they dance slowly towards the kiss waiting for them
inside the small wooden box of the evening. Red curtains,
blue walls, marigolds and marmalade. The daffodils

step gently out of their clothes
as the dark boat of oil moves south, towards ecstasy.
And ecstasy is a song that plays us,
a burning piece of real estate, not for sale.

7.

Nothing left but the bleating of frogs bleating of frogs
bleating of bad machines. Put on your shoes
of crushed dynamite and listen to me: this phone line
runs straight into the fire, directly into the green

shambling house of the sea, here's the receiver now TALK
"Take my wallet, take my stamp collection, my
toy trains, my book of Greek poets," and the sour barricade speaks
I don't want what you give, only what I take

8.

The Catholic Church burned Giordano Bruno to death
for believing the universe had no end. So some fearful Vatican
inside us craves fences, walls, air conditioning.
On his birthday I ride a train through this city in which

there is nothing that is not for sale, and see graffiti written
in the furthest reaches of the subway tunnels. I know the way
snow peas and morning glories spiral towards their god. I know
how even a grapefruit is a door some want open, some want closed.

9.

Tell me again why we are here. Tell me again
why we sold the goat to buy volume "K"
of the Encyclopedia Britannica, why the mill
squeaks like a mouse and the Horsepeople

live on the quiet mountain that has no name. Tell me
why the ambulances move from right to left
and why our President keeps the severed hands
of a violinist in a glass jar on his desk. Tell me why

10.

as he got down from his bent metal stool, as he got down
from the table on which the map was spread,
as he stepped out of his garden chair
the choir wept a broken word and he cried:

"In eighth grade my favorite room in the whole school
was the library. There was great silence there between the stacks
of books. Listen. Sometimes no one said anything
as sunlight walked through the tall windows."

I Pick Up a Hitchhiker

After a few miles, he tells me
that my car has no engine.
I pull over, and we both get out
and look under the hood.
He's right.
We don't say anything more about it
all the way to California.

LAWN SERVICE

First I hear them at the front of the house, and then they come blasting around the corner: gas-powered mowers like giant angry dustpans, snarling over the lawn as a man rides in back, standing up like a chariot driver in the Roman army. Just a few passes over the lawn and it's done, and then the weed whackers come, high-pitched and whining like small airplanes. This is gardening done as a military operation, the hill seized, the enemy decimated in a surprise attack and no prisoners taken. They would use explosives if they could. It's all over in minutes, and then the workers load the mowers back into the truck and drive away. The grass that is left continues to grow, slowly and without stopping.

"THIRTY SECONDS," SAID THE SOUNDMAN

This is no good, said the Newscaster, I'm about to lie
to all these people.

Who can say what a lie really is, said his wallet,
and why should you be worried about it?

Well, I'm the high priest of sunshine, said the Newscaster.
Kansas and Indiana come to me
to find out where they live.

"Ten seconds," said the Soundman.

No one's really out there, whispered the papers in his hands.
California and New York
are just the names of these two cameras here.

"Five seconds," said the Soundman. The cameras blinked
and opened their eyes.

"Hello California, hello New York," said the Newscaster.

Law Office

I am sitting in an adjustable chair on the 32nd floor of a skyscraper in New York City. I am typing a list of a thousand names into a computer. As I work I am listening through headphones to a recording of the journals of Cabeza de Vaca, a Spanish explorer who traveled to the United States in the 15th century. The office is air-conditioned and I am wearing a tie. A hurricane has drowned half of de Vaca's crew, and most of the rest are sick and dying of starvation on an island off the Florida Keys. The names I am entering are plaintiffs in a case against Union Carbide chemical company, and about half of them are deceased. Some filing cabinets are behind me; one is marked "Bhopal" and another reads "Breast Implants." The secretary sitting beside me goes to get a cup of coffee. De Vaca and his crew have eaten their horses, and are now sailing in a makeshift raft that uses their hides for sails. I keep typing. At noon a man comes through the office and waters all the plants. Every hour another sailor dies of pneumonia, or loses his grip and slides off the raft into the storm.

SUPERMARKET HISTORIANS

All historians should be supermarket cashiers.
Imagine what we'd learn;
"Your total comes to $10.66,
and that's the year the Normans invaded Britain."
Or, "That'll be $18.61, the year
the Civil War began."

Now all my receipts are beaches
where six-year-olds find bullets in the sand.
My tomatoes add up to Hiroshima,
and if I'd bought one more carton of milk
the cashier would be discussing the Battle of the Bulge
and not the Peloponnesian War.

But I'm tired of buying soup cans
full of burning villages,
tired of hearing the shouts of Marines
storming beaches in the bread aisle.
I want to live in a house
carved into a seed
inside a watermelon—
to look up at the red sky
as shopping carts roll through the aisles
like distant thunder.

Conversation With the Nobody

One day I was busy writing a poem
when this horse walked into my room.

But a horse did not walk into your room.

Okay one day I was writing a poem
when a lion stepped out of the wall.

But a lion did not step out of the wall.

No listen the other day I was feeding my giraffe
when this poem came up to me.

But there is no poem.

Look how can I write anything if you always
erase it, I said.

Okay.

There is a horse.
There is a lion.
There is a giraffe.

But there is still no poem.

ORGAN MUSIC

Red columns through which smoke
strays and marches, stone on stone
gathering with age a talk
full of cats' eyes, a house of bone
where we pray to the sky in which a ship
burns. Book of moon and fire,
book of the black seeds kept
within laughter, inside the voice of the choir
standing on the earth made of tears.
I place a coin on the ladder
of pain's wealth, lay my hands
on mother, father; the surf
rinses us clear to new dirt, a sound
holding the year in dark sand.

A Demonstration Against Cargill Agricultural Company

In every window of the Grain Exchange building
there is a man in a shirt and tie, looking down
at the demonstrators and their signs,
watching the Sioux Indians singing
as they beat a large drum
they carry parallel to the earth.
Across the street, two men
are tearing a building down,
one working a wrecking ball, the other
spraying water onto the wreckage
with a hose, keeping down the dust
though much of it
rises, drifting lightly
through the sun-filled air
to touch the windows
of the Grain Exchange.

Song of the Poison in the Executioner's Needle

I am all the determination of the State wrenched
into a vial, a nail for the heart, a chemical axe
for the body
and its great tree of blood.
I cannot hear radios or violins,
families, guns
or money. Do not tell me
about mother's milk, about your laws
bent towards harmony
or revenge. I could not have bandaged the cuts
the handcuffs dug in his wrists
as he struggled. I could not have said
his name. I could not have sat down beside him
and explained why it was necessary
for him to die.

NICOLLET ISLAND BONFIRE

The kids throw newspapers
onto the burning world of the bonfire
as the adults drink beer
until they fall into the bushes.
A man with a beard
and pens in his shirt pocket
takes a bunch of us over to the city power lines;
he has a fluorescent light in his hand
which he says will glow
when held near so much voltage.
But the wires are too far from us,
hanging high above the ground
like metal hornets;
his light doesn't glow,
and we end up standing in the dirt road
beneath the towers
made of scared moonlight.

When we get back to the bonfire,
a woman with long hair
who lives in a purple house
tells me about how much the island has changed.
She tells me about the new houses being built,
about the surveyor's stakes she has pulled up,
and about the seeds she has planted
in the cracks of the parking lot.
She tells me about the tourists
who come to look at the houses built in 1856;
about how much property taxes have gone up,
and about her job teaching children to read.
She tells me about all the drugs she's taken
around this bonfire, and about the grandparents
who used to sit here at night and tell stories.

Tonight, a man who is selling his house
has brought a turkey for everyone to eat.
We light fireworks that explode above the trees
and then fall, silently, onto the lots full of dirt
waiting at the end of the road
like open mouths.
My bare feet sing in the wet grass
as the guitars play,
as the coolers buzz with beers
and the river knocks in its valley.
The lilacs are in bloom.
The children go to find out what is in the dark
as the airplanes go by overhead, white as bones.

THE LIGHT ABOVE CITIES

Sitting in darkness,
I see how the light of the city
fills the clouds, rosewater light
poured into the sky
like the single body we are. It is the sum
of a million lives; a man drinking beer
beneath a light bulb, a dancer spinning
in a fluorescent room, a girl reading a book
beneath a lamp.

Yet there are others— astronomers,
thieves, lovers— whose work is only done
in darkness. Sometimes
I don't want to show these poems
to anyone, sometimes
I want to remain hidden, deep in the coals
with the one who pulls the stars
through a telescope's glass, the one who listens
for the click of the lock, the one
who kisses softly a woman's eyes.

PART FOUR

Boxes and Oceans

for Martín Prechtel

1.
Imagine how it was before music
could be recorded, before it could be kept sleeping
until the day you want to spool out its sound

with power into the repeating air. Back then
perhaps you listened quicker, and a symphony
arrived in town written on sheets of paper

like the plans for a new flower
that had to be built. You stopped in the park
when you heard it, even if it was far away.

2.
They say that thousands of years ago we lived
differently, wandering to gather all we needed
from the full-harmonied earth

that gave and gave. We lived without farms
or cities, without the clever bolts
and wrenches of agriculture, without seeds

or harvest. We died young, our bodies lacing
the ground's infinite dream. Perhaps an Eden,
motionless as a water-drop on a blade of grass.

3.

I remember a Cub Scout trip we took
to the county jail. Whoever wanted to could get
fingerprinted, an official explained a few things

and then we went down a tiled corridor
with metal bars on one side. There were men
in there. I want to say we all live in jails,

that I grew up in a building made of flags
and Scout laws, but it's not true.
We visited for an hour and then went home.

4.

All that forest was wasted on air and owls
until we got here. Those Iroquois were savages
who didn't know what to do with the land.

Any mile of earth is lost unless it's ours,
unless it's lit by the steady lamp
of our knowledge. Haul the universe

into that light, all the whales and crickets
and mountains. We will sell the water
and make money out of the trees.

5.

Behind the barbed-wire fence
the coffee-colored horse
flicks his ears. His legs

and tail are the color
of a night without stars.
Perhaps these words catch

his curved strength, perhaps now
he looks out from this poem
with his curious, autumn-brown eyes.

6.

I've read in a book about how
it used to be done: how hunter
and deer were joined in an agreement

of killing and return, life honored even
as its blood ran like rain into the dark earth.
You made an offering to the deer's

spirit, and gave thanks so the wheel of stars
would not be broken. And like the deer
you agreed to die, when your death was needed.

7.

Sometimes the lights onstage are so bright
that you can see only yourself, and almost believe
that you are the great hero in whom

all music begins. But believe that and the song
will stop breathing, becoming only a dead sugar
with which to fatten your name. Lights

out: I climb down from the stage,
from the ruined magic that should have been given
back to the dark, and to my friends.

8.

"Welcome to the Goodhue County Jail,"
the guard announced. After crossing a line
at the Prairie Island nuclear power plant

I stood in a cement room with fifteen others.
The plastic cuffs hurt until they cut them off;
then they took me away to be photographed.

Perhaps my race and gender were like free money
in there, but still I felt like a broken drum
in that last hallway, before they told me I could go.

9.

As a kid I loved to play Capture-the-Flag,
the game we played over a whole square mile
of woods, two teams divided by a line

and all of us running after each other
through the trees. A big oak tree was a jail
they put you in if you were caught. I made a few dashes

but mostly just reveled in the thunder of knowing
they could get me: my heart playing danger music
as I cruised the woods far out, never to be caught.

10.

"It is necessary for me to be imprisoned,"
Merlin said, "in a tree. It's unfortunate,
but there it is." Necessary? Unfortunate?

What was he talking about, this man who saw time
backwards, who could read tomorrow's weather
in a blade of grass? I had a vision

of standing at England's edge, of looking far out
to where the sea gives itself to something
larger. He smiled faintly and then vanished.

11.

My father had a darkroom in the basement
where once I watched in red light
as my grandfather appeared slowly

on a wet piece of paper.
We were prospectors staring
into a river's grit, the pans of chemicals

offerings to a god of shifting water
who had to be honored
before we could fix the image in its frame.

12.

Ten hours spent stuffing envelopes
in a warehouse on Broadway: I started out cheerful
but in the end just ploughed through it,

machine-like, lost in the job. All day
we wrestled thousands of envelopes
into hundreds of boxes all addressed to a bank

as distant as the moon. I left damaged
and staring, hungry for the paycheck that came in the mail
like a bag of my own blood returned.

13.
I've spent hours laboring over a song
to record it right, playing the same melody again
and again until it is good enough

to keep forever. Often my guitar hands begged
for new sounds, but I was determined
to get the ocean into a jar, to have the victory

of nailing the music down. Years later press a button
to find that river still stuck
in its honey, safe and dreamless as a stone.

14.
I think of Beethoven, stopping in a park
as the sound of a Mozart quartet drifts
through the trees; the far-away music blossoming

even as the body of the boy genius is devoured
by the dark. Sometimes I think this poem
will save me from death, from being lost finally

and forever. But these thoughts are blankets
already eaten by moths. My body is a drum
played by water and fire, its music already lost.

15.
Breathe. Let each thought
go. Our teacher says that meditation
is not an escape

from pain, not a secret ladder out
of this slaughterhouse earth. Still
we yearn for a clear heaven

of no death, as if we were light
and not gristle, meat, bone. But let it
go: no heaven. And locks on the doors.

16.
When I was two years old and visiting Florida
there was a drought. So I found
a dripping faucet by the pool, and spent the day

in watching my red plastic bucket fill
and then disastering all that rare water
over my head. I knew every drop

had to be saved, and could only be saved
in that release of cold treasure into my hair
and down my back. So I started again.

17.
Some say that our souls chose to be caught
in the lives we have, that somehow
the small spark we are needed

this particular body, this particular time
and place, this day and hour for a reason
we do not understand. Imagine each of us

as one necessary letter in an alphabet
of water, one sound in the music
only those who have been struck like bells can hear.

18.
As a girl, my mother was told by her father
to pick all the daffodils blossoming in the yard
of the deserted house next door. So

she picked every one, but bunched the flowers tight
in one hand so that crushed and starving
she brought them to her father wilted

beyond help. "It was the only time I saw him cry,"
she said. She did not need to explain to me
how a life can be kept so safe that it will die.

19.
Shut the door. Unplug the phone.
Sometimes I think I love too much
the single quiet room a writer needs

to find the world. But words are never finished
until they are spoken aloud, given away
like a haul of glittering fish

into a boat, a music answered by the applauding rain
it is right to receive. I hear water talking
on the roof, and I write it down.

PART FIVE

Man Writes Poem

This just in a man has begun writing a poem
in a small room in Brooklyn. His curtains
are apparently blowing in the breeze. We go now
to our man Harry on the scene, what's

the story down there Harry? "Well Chuck
he has begun the second stanza and seems
to be doing fine, he's using a blue pen, most
poets these days use blue or black ink so blue

is a fine choice. His curtains are indeed blowing
in a breeze of some kind and what's more his radiator
is 'whistling' somewhat. No metaphors have been written yet,
but I'm sure he's rummaging around down there

in the tin cans of his soul and will turn up something
for us soon. Hang on — just breaking news here Chuck,
there are 'birds singing' outside his window, and a car
with a bad muffler has just gone by. Yes . . . definitely

a confirmation on the singing birds." Excuse me Harry
but the poem seems to be taking on a very auditory quality
at this point wouldn't you say? "Yes Chuck, you're right,
but after years of experience I would hesitate to predict

exactly where this poem is going to go. Why I remember
being on the scene with Frost in '47, and with Stevens in '53,
and if there's one thing about poems these days it's that
hang on, something's happening here, he's just compared the curtains

to his mother, and he's described the radiator as 'Roaring deep
with the red walrus of History.' Now that's a key line,
especially appearing here, somewhat late in the poem,
when all of the similes are about to go home. In fact he seems

a bit knocked out with the effort of writing that line,
and who wouldn't be? Looks like . . . yes, he's put down his pen
and has gone to brush his teeth. Back to you, Chuck." Well
thanks Harry. Wow, the life of the artist. That's it for now,

but we'll keep you informed of more details as they arise.

Ego

Getting rid of your ego
is like trying to throw away a garbage can.
No one believes you're serious,
and the more you yell at the garbagemen
the better the neighbors
remember your name.

A Theory of Personality

There's the Gorilla and there's the Talent Agent. The Gorilla is all hairy desire to ride the roller coaster and knock the Ferris wheel screaming into the river, but the Talent Agent says "No no, we can't do that, it wouldn't look good, not here, not now," and hands him an aspirin. Sometimes the Gorilla gets his arms around the Talent Agent's neck and then the car goes squealing all over the road, into the hot dog stand, dinner gets burned, millions of dollars are spent, girls run screaming out of the hotel lobby. Other times the Talent Agent has the Gorilla chained to cement blocks and there is nothing to say; dinner is so quiet you can hear the knives clink on the plates, and no one does any finger-painting. The Gorilla is easy to love, as he eats candlesticks and plays his guitar in the backyard; but it's the Talent Agent who buys new candlesticks, who remembers how to tune the guitar. He's the one who rents the tuxedo, who shines the shoes and ties the bowtie, who gives the Gorilla his cue to walk out to the podium on the brightly-lit stage, clear his throat, and begin speaking: "I'd like to thank the Academy for this award, and to bring my agent out here, without whom none of this would have been possible." The audience applauds, flashbulbs pop, and the Gorilla and Talent Agent embrace.

JOKE

Fuck Buddhism I'm dying. Every day more cells in my body drive fast cars into brick walls. Every day new diseases are created in the dark wells of the Amazon. My only hope is ginseng and organic bananas. My only hope is dried flowers and Las Vegas. My only hope is that girl right there, the look in her eyes, the wine glass in her hand, the joke I'm about to tell.

Jazz for the Widow of Ice Cream

If I caught myself, dearly, with a thousand furies
and the red boat in the President's bath,
then the hard anchors of motor homes
would falter sleepy in the not-too-dark.

If I hugged a pigeon, midnight, the crane rope
and a taste of soup, if I burned a beacon raw
upstream, then the slow cow of swamplands
would glide gently into an avalanched room.

If you were green mirrors and a breath of salt,
if you lurked dangerously between a dry dock
and a minnow, then the smell of music would dim
and the ship knock in its port without a bell.

We earn reflectively our newest keys. The donkey
manages his own hurrah, and the calm zipper of sunlight
folds its cards. This again, slowly, no bridge
and the slow hoot of the ocean going home.

MAN IN A LIGHTED ROOM AT SUNDOWN

To him is denied the soft bewilderment of dusk,
the slow drifting of his room out to sea.
He doesn't see the shadows joining hands to become the night,
the question of noon unraveling behind a chair.

Instead he knows a room bright as an eagle's eye, lit by a lamp
that is all yes or no. Yet as he lies down to sleep
the requiems between the stars move closer
to rush in, as he clicks the switch, like the dark ideas of thieves.

Van Gogh: "Self-Portrait with Straw Hat" and "Woman Peeling Potatoes"

With long looking into himself
he found a face that is a swirl of yellow and red spinning
around the hungry, determined centers
of his eyes. And behind that face,
on the other side of the wooden board
from which he stares, he painted

a large peasant woman
peeling potatoes by candlelight
into a metal pail. Perhaps
the storm-and-sunshine of his soul
had her at its center; perhaps
when the unhappy, bandaged one
went out to the cornfield with a pistol
and a head full of jagged darkness
it was she who whispered *no home, no home*
as a potato fell into the pail
like a lost shard of the moon.

Subway at Rush Hour

The slim Asian woman
with long black hair
gets off at Grand Street

I feel the warmth
her hand has left
on the metal pole

CIRCE
Odyssey, Book X

After she turned my men into pigs
she sat down beside me,
the air around her body crackling
with voltage and butterflies.
Then she picked up the glass
of black honey
and placed it into my hands,
weaving me into her stare
as she spoke in a voice
that could have opened a stone, saying *drink*

MOSAIC

With your beautiful hands you showed me
how to smash a tile with a hammer
to break shards enough
to make a picture whole. Now
if I could just get this clay square to split
in a gentle curve
I could finish this pattern I've started
of a green guitar. It's a puzzle half made
and half destroyed, an accident I let happen
as the hammer cracks on the tile
like the first day of school, like that shattering cut
the knife made
through the umbilical cord.
Months after our first kiss,
each of us slowly learns where the other
has been broken. Together
our lives make a pattern
neither of us could have planned.

In Summer

We stood naked in the grass, ice-cold water spilling
out of the green hose you held, water

that bit me numb, that rattled and satisfied.
Dried mud ran from my shoulders and chest.

If we said anything then it was lost
in the hot noise of August, in the buzzing

of the cornfield around us. No one but me
could see how your body shone

as you reached out gently to brush
the last dirt from my arm. Your eyes

avoided mine. Do you
remember? We stood there a moment

dripping in the hot sun
and then you dropped the hose into the grass.

Her Name Written in Pencil on the Wall Beside the Phone

I spent hours at the sandwich board in a dirty apron
slicing baguettes with a long knife, arranging tomatoes
and onions, basil and provolone and peppers and mustard
and goat cheese, eating hummus in full view of the security camera
from which the boss often watched. Pots of chili simmered
as the gray-haired dishwasher hauled clattering racks of plates
out of a steaming aluminum box, as the baker
sprinkled powdered sugar on lemon bars, as the radio blared
and the mixer groaned. Slips of green paper scrawled
with sandwich orders lighted like insects
on every available surface around me. Bacon popped
and cracked on the grill, rain on a hot street.

On my break I threw my apron into the laundry bag
and rushed across the street to her apartment
above the record store, pushing the cracked plastic doorbell
until she came lightly down the stairs. It was that first month
when it seemed neither of us could survive very long
without the other, when we would leave town suddenly
to lie down in long grass. She opened the door, her brown eyes
singing beneath her red hair. We had one hour.
Upstairs she lit candles to convince us both
that we did not have jobs, that there was only
music, a room full of paintings, a song beyond clothes,
beyond her glasses set gently on the table. My hands
in her long hair, the two of us swaying
in the warm hum below our names.

Then the hurting clock pulled me towards money,
towards the white plastic handle of the knife
on the cutting board. In her saffron scarf

she went with me, walking across the street
to the white brick corner of the bakery
where we hid our kisses from the large windows,
from the green plastic chairs and the lights strung
in the linden trees. Autumn of leaves and voices.
Autumn of Jennifer and her enormous laugh.
She walked back to the corner
and I went in to bleach and coffee, to sugar
howling in the cakes. The espresso machine
banged. Taste of her lips. Wheel
of hunger and bread and sleep.

GRANDPA PUTTING SALT
ON HIS ICE CREAM

He would hold the salt shaker
in his right hand, and tap the end
over the dark chocolate.
"It enhances the flavor," he would say.
He had more ice cream in his life
than his ancestors ever did, and more butter,
and more milk, and more eggs.
And when these things filled his veins
and pulled him down,
when the barn of his heart caught fire,
it was those ancestors that his eyes
rolled back to see;
strong Norwegian brothers
driving their cows out of the fields
towards the market and the city,
towards railroads and electric lights,
towards world wars and cameras,
towards his body, his thoughts
and his life.

SUGARHOUSE

After the funeral, my mother and her sister
were caught for days in the sugarhouse
of their parent's belongings, sorting through dishes
and clothes, tables and chairs, dividing much of it
between them, throwing some things out, giving
others away and setting the dearest things aside
to be divided later. In this way
they boiled the house down
until they were left with two last
precious things: the maple syrup pitcher
and the sugar bowl. As if
after childhood was poured away
each vessel was still sweet
from years of caring, though empty now.

SHE KILLED THE SPIDER
for Robert Bly

She killed the spider
that I've been watching all summer,
the one whose grey bedsheets flapped
in the corner beside the mailbox.
I liked coming home
to that web spun by the door,
to the spider hiding in the corner
and the gnats caught in the web
like mail.

Now it's autumn, and the nights are cold.
I value every name
in my address book
even more.

DRIVING A RETARDED GIRL TO LAKE MINNETONKA

Even if I had been there
when you were three years old,
I'm not sure
I could have prevented your father
from hitting you with a baseball bat.
The long drive I take us on
is all I can do
to keep you and the world safe.
Buckled into the front seat,
you can't take off your clothes
or flush magazines and shoes down the toilet.
When we get to the lake, it has gone silver
in the sunset all summer was made for,
and the cheap song on the radio
almost has me in tears.
How much is decided for us
before we are born,
before we can say "No."
You do not want to get out of the van
and I cannot leave you alone.
I drive us home, and tell myself
you know we have done more
than nothing at all.

Scrubbing a Pan

While scrubbing a pan I remember

pedaling my green bicycle late at night
through snow-buried streets

towards the theater of warm darkness
where the snow melted from my boots

and the muse beckoned
from the beer-soaked stage

as the guitarist pounded heaven
into my chest

That song remained
after I showered the smoke out of my hair

and the ringing faded from my ears
Ten years, one city, and nine apartments later

in a small yellow kitchen
with water running over my hands

I can still hear it

Moving Away

My guitar sings
until the pictures come off the walls
and the money in my wallet starts to burn. Boxes
have swallowed my home, and the window of my car
can only be opened with a wrench.
I must sell everything, until all I own
is the day I will leave. Our tears
remember everyone we have loved. There is no kiss
which does not lift a house off the ground.

SECRET RIVER

There are new paintings
beyond the old paintings.
There are new songs
beyond the old songs.
We are all touching
inside the secret river.
There are new words
beyond these words.

Acknowledgments

I am very grateful to the following publications, in which poems from *Dynamite on a China Plate* first appeared: *Barbaric Yawp, Ritter Oleander, Euphony, Goodfoot, Heliotrope, Lilliput Review, Luna, Minnesota Monthly, Mudfish, Northwest Review, Ploughshares, Poet Lore, Poetry East, Rattapallax, Release* and *The Thousands*.

This book would not be what it is without the contributions of many others beside myself. I would like to thank my family for their encouragement and support, and to honor and remember my father, Joseph Leeming, and his love of language. I would especially like to thank Robert Bly, whose encouragement and example have been a great gift to me. I honor and thank Martín Prechtel, whose teachings have deeply nourished these words. I thank Craig Ungerman and the members of the Minnesota Sufi group, for giving these poems their first home. I offer my thanks and praises to the community of the Minnesota Men's Conference, which gave these poems a house to dance in. I remember and thank the former members of Joy Buzzer and The Diving Bells, who know the crossroads where music and words meet: John Koski, Greg Thompson, John Oberg and Jeff Summers. I thank Charles Bowe for his laughter and his firecracker mind. I thank my grandfather Howard James Lee for planning ahead. I thank my fellow poets and friends Timothy Young, Thomas R. Smith and Matthew Thorburn for their willingness to look under the hood of the poetic car. I thank David Lehman and everyone in the New School University class of

2001, for keeping language alive amidst the tall buildings. I thank the community of the Great Mother Conference for their warm welcome which nourishes me still. I thank Inge Hindel for her open heart. I thank Li-Young Lee for his commitment to what is beyond ourselves, and Gioia Timpanelli for the gift of her stories. I honor and praise Fran Quinn, the open-hearted poetic strategist of heaven. I thank Barbara Miles, Shirley Colletti, and Frank and Jan Asch for their commitment to beauty. I thank all my friends on the land-locked island of Ithaca, especially Charles Orrange and Meg Elliott. I also thank Greg Kosmicki and Richard Rosenbaum, for guiding this book into being. Thanks to all those individuals who appear in these poems. Thanks and praises to all other contributors to this book, whether divine, unknown, or forgotten.

CPSIA information can be obtained at www.ICGtesting.com

261486BV00002B/1/A